Family

Family is the last and greatest discovery...
It is our last miracle.

[JAMES McBRIDE]

M·I·L·K™

MOMENTS INTIMACY LAUGHTER KINSHIP

This edition published in 2007 by WPL, The Perfume Factory,
140 Wales Farm Road, London W3 6UG.
www.wpl.eu.com

Edited and designed by WPL
Printed in China

ISBN 978-1-904264-50-7

Inspired by the 1950s landmark photographic exhibition, "The Family of Man", M.I.L.K. began as an epic global search to develop a collection of extraordinary and geographically diverse images portraying humanity's Moments of Intimacy, Laughter and Kinship (M.I.L.K.). This search took the form of a photographic competition – probably the biggest and almost certainly the most ambitious of its kind ever to be conducted. Chosen from 40,000 entries worldwide, the 300 winning images cut across race and nationality and celebrate what it is to be part of a family, to share the gift of friendship and more than anything else, to be loved.

These photographs were first published as three books entitled "Family", "Friendship" and "Love" in early 2001 and are now featured in a range of products worldwide, in nine different languages in more than 20 countries.

M·I·L·K

Each individual is a marvellous

opportunity.

[DALAI LAMA]

Making the decision to have a child is momentous.
It is to decide forever to have your heart go
walking around outside your body.

[ELIZABETH STONE]

The family is one of nature's masterpieces.

[GEORGE SANTAYANA]

Parents hold their children's hands a while
and their hearts forever.

[AUTHOR UNKNOWN]

Oh what a power is motherhood.

[EURIPIDES]

Wherever mum is, that's where home is.

[FELICITY MARTIN]

When a child is born, a father is born.

[FREDERICK BUECHNER]

Hold tenderly that which you cherish.

[BOB ALBERTI]

There are two things we must give our children.

One is roots and the other is wings.

[HODDING CARTER]

If you can give your son or daughter only
one gift, let it be enthusiasm.

[BRUCE BARTON]

Seek the wisdom of the ages,

but look at the world through

the eyes of a child.

[RON WILD]

The one thing children wear out
faster than shoes is parents.

[JOHN J. PLOMP]

When our relatives are at home, we have to

think of all their good points or it would be

impossible to endure them.

[GEORGE BERNARD SHAW]

Brothers and sisters are
as close as hands and feet.

[VIETNAMESE PROVERB]

Chance made us sisters,
time made us friends.

[ANON]

A sister is both your mirror and your opposite.

A brother is a friend given by nature.

[FRENCH PROVERB]

Families are like fudge...

mostly sweet with a few nuts.

[ANON]

Family faces are magic mirrors.
Looking at people who belong to us,
we see the past, present, and future.

[GAIL LUMET BUCKLEY]

Never have children,
only grandchildren.

[GORE VIDAL]

Mothers bear children.

Grandmothers *enjoy* them.

[SPANISH PROVERB]

In every conceivable manner,

the family is a link to our past,

a bridge to our future.

[ALEX HALEY]

When you look at your life,

the greatest happinesses are

family happinesses.

[AUTHOR UNKNOWN]

Call it a clan, call it a network,
call it a tribe, call it a family.
Whatever you call it, whoever you are,
you need one.

[ANON]

IMAGES

The beautiful mountain scenery of Zanskar in the
Indian Himalayas is the setting for a twilight stroll.
In a region which is snow-covered for the most of the
year, Norbu and his young granddaughter make the
most of the warm sunshine.
© Andrei Jewell

The Gobi Desert, Mongolia – stranded with all of their
belongings, a nomadic family are relaxed as they await
help.
© Luca Trovato

Cheek to cheek – father and daughter hold each other
close on a chilly morning in Gaspésie, Quebec, Canada.
© Dave Marcheterre

Bath time – Maryland, USA.
© David MacNeill

One-month-old Malik is the centre of attention for his loving parents, Cecile and Hafid, photographed at their home in Villeurbaine, France.
© Slim Labidi

A quiet moment – parents Kevin and Annette tenderly embrace 10-month-old Jai during a family photo session in Bellingen, Australia.
© Georgina Lucock

Mother and baby, New Zealand.
© Emma Bass

Like mother, like daughter – at a New York airport, there's still time for nine-month-old Verity and her mother Lydzia to play before the long flight home to England.
© Stefano Azario

Mother and son captured on film in Butuo County, Sichuan province, China.
© Jia Lin Wu

The simple love of a family bonds a father and son beside the Fiherenana river in Madagascar. The Malagasy people come to this area to mine for sapphires.
© Louise Gubb

Front and back – in the Cameron Highlands, Malaysia, a mother carries her children in the traditional way of the Orang Asli people.
© Guan Cheong Wong

Taking flight – Washington, USA.
© Pat Justis

Brother and sister – six-year-old Ethan gives
four-year-old Emory an enthusiastic hug at a
birthday party in Brooklyn, New York.
© David M. Grossman

Father and son captured at the Goldstone soccer
ground in Hove, England.
© Kris Allan

Open wide – on a trip to the beach in Wellfleet,
Massachusetts, USA, nothing interests Zane more than
her mother, Susan.
© Neil Selkirk

During a family photo session in Altrincham, Cheshire,
England, one-year-old Philip looks unimpressed by the
behaviour of his older sister, Alice.
© Sefton Samuels

The family bond begins at an early age for a young brother and sister in Lancang, China.
© Jia Lin Wu

Two of a kind – the photographer's great-aunts at their home in Canada. Sisters Rose and Florence have lived together since they were both widowed in their 40s.
© Andrew Danson

An inseparable pair – elderly Ukrainian sisters caught on film during a visit to Cleveland, Ohio, USA.
© Bernard Mendoza

Sibling hug, England.
© Zoe Ali

In tandem – a novel way of moving house captured on film in Miami Beach, Florida, USA.
© Bill Frakes

A grandmother's gaze – as she joins her family in celebrating her granddaughter's wedding in Brisbane, Australia.
© Stephen McAlphine

Overcoming the generation gap in Brummen, the Netherlands. Eighty-one years separate a grandfather from his only grandchild, but that's no barrier to play. Two-year-old Jarón chooses the game.
© Guus Rijven

The surprise party – a grandmother delights in the company of her grandchildren as she celebrates her 85th birthday in Yakima, Washington, USA.
© Deborah Roundtree

Keeping tradition alive near Lake San Pablo, Ecuador.
Four generations of an Imbabura Indian family prepare
their hair in the time-honoured way – from right to left:
Mama-Rosa, Rosa, Rosa Elena and Miriam.
© Juan P. Barragán

A great-grandmother's heartfelt embrace of a young
bride. The old lady, 97, and her great-granddaughter
are the only family members who still live in the
mountain village of Roccaspinalveti, Italy.
© Roberto Colacioppo

Another generation learns about mustering from the
head of the family. "Big" Morrie Dingle, a grazier in
South Queensland, Australia, and his two grandsons
take a break from the saddle to enjoy some food.
© Ray Peek